T0158302

PENGUIN BUSINESS

TWENTY-FIVE SMALL HABITS

Manoj Chenthamarakshan is an educator, author and the founder of The Positive Store, an e-commerce platform formed in 2018 to help people lead a positive and productive life. At the age of twenty-two, he got a well-paying job and successfully became a graphic designer. He earned his dream bike and lived the lifestyle that he dreamt of. But then came a day when he was invited to a party. He was asked to introduce himself. He was not happy with the title of graphic designer. This incident made him think about his identity. Later, he decided to figure out his passion and purpose. He knew that he couldn't find it by staying on the job. So he decided to quit his job and go on a solo trip to north India. After two years of research and self-exploration, he realized that he was surrounded by great books, such as *The Secret*, *Think and Grow Rich* and *The Power of Your Subconscious Mind*. Everything started connecting when he looked backwards. This awareness helped him to discover NLP (neuro-linguistic programming). He completed the course in Bangalore and worked as a trainer for a year. Knowledge was in abundance, but the results were poor. It took him a few years to realize that knowledge is of no use if it is not practised. He later decided to structure his life and started creating planners, bringing in his accumulated knowledge throughout the years. Thus formed The Positive Store. They have currently sold more than 50,000 products worldwide. During this journey as an entrepreneur, he also found his passion in expressing his ideas through words, which made him write books such as *Twenty-Five Small Habits*, *Fifty-Five Questions to Ask Yourself* and *Know Thyself*, which are available on Amazon.

3. MEDITATING

*'If every eight-year-old in this world is taught
meditation, we will eliminate violence from the world
within one generation.'*

—Dalai Lama

Meditation is a great way to transform your mind. Let
us look at how it does this.

How Meditation Affects Your Brain

When you meditate, your brain stops processing
information as actively as it normally would. Beta
waves (a kind of brain waves that dominate our
consciousness when we direct attention towards
cognitive tasks) tend to decrease, which is an
indication that the brain is processing information.
This happens even after a short meditation session
and even if you've never attempted it before.

This is what really happens in individual brain parts:

- The frontal lobe is the most evolved brain area that is responsible for planning, reasoning, self-conscious awareness and emotions. It goes offline during meditation.
- The parietal lobe is responsible for processing sensory information concerning the world, orienting you in space and time. The activity in this area slows down during meditation.
- The thalamus, which is also known as the gatekeeper for your senses, funnels sensory data deep into your brain to focus your attention and, in the process, stop other signals in their tracks. Meditation decreases the flow of incoming info to a drip.
- The reticular formation is the brain's sentry or the structure that receives incoming stimuli before placing the brain on high alert, all set to respond. Meditation sort of dials back the arousal signal.

With these changes taking place in your brain, these are the benefits you get to enjoy:

- A Better Sense of Self-Awareness
  Meditation lets you take an inventory of your body mentally. *How is your body feeling in the present moment? What are the amazing things your body can do? Are you feeling weak or strong? What can*

you do to heal or remedy that which is aching in your body?

So, much like yoga, meditation helps you create a better connection between your body and mind. Through this better sense of self-awareness, you are able to cultivate the present-moment awareness that lets you remain in the present, grounded and well-focused in all aspects and each moment of your life.

- Less Anxiety and Stress
  Obsessing over the future or the past can often make you unhappy. When you are totally immersed in the present moment, you are content. You can only control what is taking place in this moment, which is why you don't have a reason to be caught up in the past or remain absorbed in the future.

  Your life is fully in the now, and meditation is the anchor to assist you to stay there. It is the key to reducing stress, having control over your anxiety and, ultimately, leading a happier, stress-free life.

Other benefits include the following:

- More mental clarity
- Enhanced emotional intelligence
- Better memory
- More compassion
- More creativity

And there are many more!

Exercise

Set aside about fifteen minutes of your time every day to meditate. You can start with this simple process:

1. Lie or sit comfortably on a mat or cushion.
2. Close your eyes. Don't try to control your breath, just breathe as you would naturally do.
3. Focus your attention on your breath as well as on the way your body moves with every inhalation and exhalation. Notice the way your body moves as you breathe. Take note of your shoulders, chest, belly and rib cage. Just focus on your breath without making any effort to control its intensity or pace. Your mind may wander in the process. When it happens, gently return your focus back to your breath.
4. If you are meditating for the first time, do it for two to three minutes before gradually extending the span.

4. NATURE-GAZING

'Nature always wears the colors of the spirit.'

—Ralph Waldo Emerson

Nature-gazing is a kind of meditation that can be practised in many ways. As the name suggests, nature-gazing encompasses spending some time connecting your gaze to any aspect of nature. This could be a stream, waterfall, grass, trees, stars, clouds or even animals. With nature-gazing, you get all the benefits of meditation that we mentioned earlier.

In the 1980s, Stephen and Rachel Kaplan conducted a study of the effects of nature on people. They discovered that small glimpses of nature, or access to 'nearby nature', had profound, measurable psychological effects which improve the well-being of people. Actually, even a small, trivial sight, like a couple of trees observed through a window, could still engender a great feeling.

The Kaplans found that people who have access to greater natural settings were generally healthier than those who didn't. What's more, these people also reported experiencing better levels of satisfaction in terms of their job, home and other important aspects of life.

As an example, let's look at how you can practise sky-gazing meditation.

This is one of the most commonly practised nature-gazing methods. You can either do it indoors or outdoors within a few minutes.

Exercise

Anytime you feel mentally cluttered and mentally fatigued, or just overwhelmed, practise this meditation technique. It will help you to get refreshed and centred, quieting your busy mind. When you are done, you'll be feeling more refreshed, ready to focus, concentrate and think.

How to Do It

1. Find a high area from where you can get a good view of the vast clear sky (a flat place on the ground that is not close to any obstructions is also fine).
2. Sit comfortably (you can also lie down) and calm your mind for a short period of time as you take long, deep and slow breaths.
3. Tilt your head a little upwards, making sure you assume a good posture, and gaze into the clear blue sky.

4. Let all of your thoughts go, release all fear, uncertainty, doubt, sadness . . . basically, anything that has been bothering you. Release it all into the sky that is spacious and large enough to accommodate all the worries in the world. Let them all pass by like clouds. Encourage your awareness to unite slowly with the vast blue sky.

5. Take note of the way your inner thoughts are evaporating into your inner sky, just like the clouds evaporating in the sky. Notice that this expansive, open experience is essentially the most important and natural state of your being.

6. Hold on to this state for as long as you can, and when you get distracted, go back to it gently.

5. WORKING OUT

'Physical fitness is not only one of the most important keys to a healthy body, it is the basis of dynamic and creative intellectual activity.'

—John F. Kennedy

Exercising is important. Everyone knows that. You need to make exercise a habit in your life for optimal physical and mental health. Contrary to what most of us think, exercising does not just help with weight loss and the prevention/ management of chronic diseases. It also has the following benefits:

- ***Gives you better mental clarity***
  Exercising boosts energy levels and increases the neurotransmitter known as serotonin, which leads to mental clarity and, in consequence, improved productivity.

- *Makes you happier*
  There are many studies that show that exercising generates happy emotions, owing to the release of chemicals in the brain, which include endorphins, norepinephrine, dopamine and serotonin. These tend to improve mood, alleviate pain and relieve stress.

- *Makes you look better*
  Exercising not only makes you look shredded or lean, it tends to increase blood flow to the skin, something which makes sure that oxygen and nutrients that generally improve skin health and heal wounds are delivered to different parts of the body faster. By training properly, experts assert, you get to add more blood vessels to your skin. All of this leads to better-looking and healthier skin.

Other scientifically proven benefits of exercising include:

- Improves your muscles and bones
- Increases your energy levels
- Reduces your chances of getting various chronic diseases, such as type-2 diabetes
- Improves your confidence and self-esteem
- Boosts your memory
- Helps with relaxation and improves sleep quality

Exercise

I know you already have dozens of ideas about working out, but I would suggest that you keep it simple and enjoy it. Also, unless you are a pro athlete who's been strength-training for years, I would recommend that you select a full-body routine that you can do three or so times per week (depending on your schedule).

You want to have a regimen that includes at least an exercise for the legs (quads, which is the front leg area, and hamstrings, which is the rear leg area) and butts; an exercise that involves your 'pull' muscles and one that involves your 'push' muscles; and another one for the core.

More specifically, you can start with the following breakdown if you don't want to stick to the usual jogging, sit-ups, jumping jacks, walking exercises. In other words, if you want to have more targeted movements, try the following sample exercises:

- *For quads*: squats, box jumps, lunges
- *For hamstrings and butts*: deadlifts, hip raises, step-ups and good-mornings
- *Push exercises for shoulders*: bench press, push-ups, incline dumbbell press and overhead press
- *Pull exercises for biceps, forearms and back*: body-weight rows, dumbbell rows, chin-ups and pull-ups
- *Core exercises for lower back and abs*: exercise-ball crunches, planks, jumping knee tucks, mountain-climbers and hanging leg raises

All you have to do now is pick one or two exercises from each category above and you'll cover nearly all the muscles in your body. Please seek advice and direction from your local fitness instructor for exercises that you are not familiar with.

Finally, one hour is enough to complete a workout. If that is too much, thirty minutes, too, are good enough.

6. EATING HEALTHIER

The benefits of healthy eating are pretty obvious. When you eat healthy food, you have more energy, better weight, better health, which translate to more productivity—you are able to think and generally feel better.

Healthy eating also plays a role in reducing the risk of many diseases and in managing nearly all of them. I am talking about diseases and conditions like type-2 diabetes, cancer, high blood pressure, cardiovascular diseases and so forth.

In other words, healthy eating is everything. That's why we are often told that we are what we eat. But why is it difficult to stick to a healthy diet? There are countless reasons why this is so, but if you ask me, one of the main reasons is simply *your environment*.

The Role of the Environment

Your behaviour is largely shaped by your environment, and thus, what you eat is easily defined by your environment. What you eat on a daily basis is determined by what is presented to you.

There was a research paper published in the *American Journal of Public Health*, conducted by Anne Thorndike, a physician at the Massachusetts General Hospital, Boston. Together with her colleagues, she changed what is known as the 'choice architecture' (this means changing the manner in which food and drinks are displayed) of drinks in a cafeteria.

For this study, the three main refrigerators in a cafeteria were filled with soda. But the researchers added water in all of those bottles and placed baskets of bottled water throughout the room.

In just three months, the number of sodas sold reduced by 11.4 per cent, while the water sales increased by 25.8 per cent. The same adjustments and outcomes were recorded with various food options.

Exercise

Usually, when you are worn out, it is not really possible to go through all the effort it requires to prepare a healthy meal. You just grab what is nearest. To ensure that you always opt for healthy food, it is advisable to stock your fridge and pantry with healthy foods such as:

- Fresh fruits
- Whole grains
- Nuts and seeds
- Fresh vegetables
- Legumes
- Lean proteins

7. EMULATING A ROLE MODEL

'In order to carry a positive action, we must develop here a positive vision.'

—Dalai Lama

Having someone you admire and look up to can motivate you to achieve great feats and do amazing things. Therefore, it is critical that you have a role model. When you identify a role model who does the things you aspire to do, you are bound to take big steps of growth. Most of our greatest ideas come from seeing what our heroes did or have been doing. Therefore, you should try as much as possible to pattern your behaviour after them.

If you don't have a role model, let me give you examples of some role models who have had a great impact on my life.

1. Theodore Roosevelt. This is my greatest role model in American history. This man's life has taught me

a lot about character. He lived boldly, speaking his mind freely, and ensured he backed up his words with solid actions laden with conviction and purpose.

Roosevelt conducted his affairs with respect for other people and with dignity. Indeed, he was legendary for the way he carried himself, as well as for his kindness and graciousness, which deserve emulation. According to him: *'Character in the long run, is the decisive factor in the life of a person.'*

2. Roger Federer. This tennis player is my role model for many reasons. Firstly, he loves what he does, and that's why he maintains his standing as one of the best players in the world. Federer does not need any other motivation than just being there in the moment and doing what he was born to do.

He loves to show up at all tennis tournaments and compete fiercely with anyone who is willing to challenge him. I think his competitive greatness is simply legendary. His career story inspires and motivates me to go to work every day and do an awesome job.

Exercise

Choose Your Role Models

First of all, you have to look around for each and every quality that inspires you. If you find a person who has these qualities and you can reach them, approach them in whichever manner and ask them questions such as:

How exactly do you do it? How can I follow in your footsteps?

If, perhaps, the person is not reachable (like Roosevelt), just look up their memoirs, biographies, and the books and articles about them, or any other material that describes them and how they live (or lived) their lives.

When You Find a Role Model, Listen to Them

You chose them as a role model for a reason. You were able to resonate with their ideas or vision, or their character. What you see in them is the reflection of yourself. Make sure you follow them on a regular basis. This will help you to stay on track. As human beings, we get distracted easily. By following your role models on a regular basis, you are realigning with your goals and visions.

8. READING

'To earn more, you must learn more.'

—Brian Tracy

We are usually advised to develop a habit and culture of reading. However, for some people, it is easy to do this, because it is probably a hobby for them, while for others, it is boring and tedious.

I used to hate reading books, because I didn't exactly know how I would gain from them. After *too many people* advised me to start reading for myriads of reasons, I decided to look into this area on my own. These are the main reasons why I have come to love reading:

You Are Exposed to Fresh Things

Through a culture of reading, you get exposure and info about so much: new ways of solving problems, new ways of achieving certain goals; how to think, how to become happier, how to be contented with life and grow in your career, what is happening around you . . . The list is simply endless.

Self-Improvement

Reading different material helps you become a better person, especially because you get to understand how the environment around you operates and how different people think.

You come across important information that helps you develop as a person, whether in business or in relationships, in school and parenting, among other things. Different books are like different classes in a school taught by different experts in their own unique fields, attending which, at the end of the day, leaves you more knowledgeable and equipped with better skills in different facets of life.

Improves Your Understanding of Life

Basically, the more you read, the more you understand the many aspects of life, and the better placed you become to navigate the world more easily. Let's take a look at one example here.

Reading multiple psychology books, about behaviour traits and things like that, gives you a better understanding of how different people react to or view certain behavioural practices and tendencies. It enables you to understand why people behave the way they do, and how best to approach different people and how to treat them.

Generally, you also understand the rules of life through reading. You know what is expected of you in society and what is not.

There are so many other reasons why you should read books, which are nearly the same as why people go to school. Appreciating this fact is important when you want to cultivate a habit of reading and stick to it.

Remember that most successful people have this one common trait: they educate themselves on a regular basis. They would never tell you that they are done gaining knowledge.

Exercise

Once you get some books, keep them in your workspace or on the bedside table, to remind yourself to read daily.

If you have come this far, then I guess you would love my other books as well. Check out *Fifty-Five Questions to Ask Yourself*, *Comfortable Slaves* and *Know Thyself*.

9. WRITING DOWN YOUR IDEAS

I have always thought that a successful life is one in which you are able to constantly turn thoughts into successful actions. All of us have many thoughts, and many of us, unfortunately, let them slip away before taking any action on them.

One very important step, between having a thought and translating it into successful action, is to bring a thought from within you to the outside. A good way to do this is by writing it down. Whatever the thought is, writing it down does have a lot of benefits, because your brain then begins taking it very seriously. Let us learn some benefits of writing down your thoughts.

Benefits of Jotting Ideas Down

- The idea becomes more cemented in your brain.
- When you write a thought down, you are able to consider the goal and the obstacles clearly, isolated

from the emotions that they were tangled up in before you wrote your thought down. Again, if it's an obstacle, you are now able to see whether the situation is the same as what you've experienced in the past, which means that you can use the previous experience to overcome the obstacle.

- You are now better able to brainstorm on a more ambitious level. If you think about it, you cannot write down a start-up idea in the middle of a blank page and then begin branching out with a burst of ideas.

- What's more, writing down your thoughts enables you to explore your dreams that you may not be wishing to share with other people. It also gives you the physical space to track those thoughts and go back to them later if required.

- You get to learn more. In 2010, a study conducted by Indiana University discovered that the areas in the brains of children connected with learning operated so much better when the children were asked to jot down words such as 'spaceship' on their own as opposed to reading the words on a whiteboard. Therefore, note-taking in class, after all, was not all for nothing.

- It clears your mental RAM and enables you to remain sharper as you age. Did you know that your brain is like a hard drive? Well, the brain is multilayered, very complex and super epic. The process of writing down ideas, emotions and thoughts helps your brain to unload some baggage, providing it with more room to think about other stuff. I'd also say that all the extra space that's created makes you relax, but I think you've guessed that already. Furthermore, writing your thoughts down helps keep you on top of your memory game longer. This is according to the science journal *Neurology*. The study's author states that doing such an activity across your lifetime exercises the brain and thus ensures that its health is sustained for longer.

Exercise

Simply buy a journal and keep it in your workspace. Write, write, write . . .

10. GOAL WRITING

'The key to success is to focus our conscious mind on things we desire, not things we fear.'

—Brian Tracy

Dr Gail Matthews, a professor of psychology at Dominican University, California, conducted a study on goal-setting with 267 participants. This study found that by writing down your goals, you are 42 per cent more likely to achieve them.

Definitely, most of us don't bother writing down our goals; instead, we aimlessly drift through life, wondering why our lives lack significance and purpose. I am not saying that the endgame is committing to your goals by jotting them down. This is only the beginning. The secret to achieving anything that matters most to you is making an effort to write down your goals. This is crucial for the following reasons.

It Clarifies What It Is That You Want

Just imagine setting out on a trip without having any specific destination in mind. How do you pack? What roads do you use? How exactly do you know when you've arrived?

Instead, how about you start by picking your destination?

This applies to the milestones in your life, too. When you write down your goals, you are forced to choose something specific and determine what you want.

It Motivates You to Take Action

Jotting down your goals is just the beginning. It is important to articulate your intention, but that is not enough. You have to execute your goals. You have to take action. When I write down my goals and review them every now and then, I am naturally triggered to take the most necessary action.

It Provides a Filter for More Opportunities

The more success you get, the more opportunities come your way. As a matter of fact, such new opportunities can become distractions real quick and can drive you off course. The best way I can think of to manage this is maintaining a list of well-written goals, by which you can evaluate these fresh opportunities.

It Assists You in Overcoming Resistance

Each important dream, intention or objective comes across as resistance. From the moment you set a goal and write it down, you'll start feeling it. If you, however, focus on the resistance, it only becomes stronger. The best way to overcome it is by looking at the written goal—the thing you really want.

It Lets You See and Celebrate Your Progress

Life is hard, but it gets worse when you cannot see any progress. This is when you begin feeling that you are working yourself to death, moving nowhere. However, written goals are much like highway mile-markers. They assist you to see how far you've come and how far you have to go. They also give you a chance to celebrate when you accomplish something.

Exercise

Get a new journal and start writing your goals clearly on a daily basis.

11. VISION BOARD GAZING

'Visualization is the human being's vehicle to the future—good, bad or indifferent. It's strictly in our control.'

—Earl Nightingale

A vision board is a collection of images that resonate with your end goal. Taking some time during the day to gaze at a vision board is a very important habit you should take up for self-development. By gazing at the vision board on a daily basis, you make your subconscious realize what your goals are.

But can you gaze at something you don't have? If you don't have one already, let's make sure you know why having a vision board is important.

The simple act of having a space where you have displayed what you want brings, in a way, that thing to life. When you have a vision board in a place where you can see it often, it makes you want to take action to achieve your goals.

Note that visualization has been termed one of the strongest exercises for the mind that you can do. There is a popular book entitled *The Secret* that points out that:

> The law of attraction is forming your entire life experience and it is doing that through your thoughts. When you are visualizing, you are emitting a powerful frequency out into the Universe.

As you ruminate on that, let's take a look at some of the benefits of having and gazing at a personal vision board.

Increased Focus

The so-called shiny object syndrome is real. You begin with good intentions on something and, sooner or later, something else appears and steals your attention, and then, all of a sudden, you are doing that thing instead. A vision board is bound to keep you focused. It assists you in remaining on course when something else is vying for your attention.

Brings Inspiration

When you create a vision board, you include in it images and words that inspire you. There are many other ways of getting inspiration, I agree, but most of these only serve to offer strong inspiration at the beginning; this is before something happens and you start losing that inspiration.

On those difficult days when you are experiencing a lot of discouragement, only a vision board can remind you of how you felt when your levels of hope were soaring and nothing felt unmanageable.

Creates Motivation

When you first start out on something, you get to experience so much excitement. However, that excitement inevitably wanes, and you begin losing motivation. Gazing at your vision board can act as a catalyst to fire up your motivation; it can prevent you from getting stuck and keep you moving forward.

It's an Incentive to Accomplish

Most successful folks let their intuition guide them when they create their boards; they use the boards to achieve a particular goal. These people place their goal on the board in their own way, which they deem best, to make it clear and visible. Gazing at it every now and then offers them the incentive to take action to reach this goal.

Exercise

Create a vision board today on your computer, phone, office wall, bedroom wall, refrigerator door or in any other area that you frequently visit or where you spend time.

What to Place There?

You can include anything that motivates or inspires you. The purpose of a vision board is to bring everything you place on it to life. Firstly, think about your goals in areas such as career, relationships, home, finance, travel and personal growth, including social life, education, spirituality and health.

Take a mental inventory of what you'd want each of these areas to look like and jot your goals down. You should always handwrite your goals as opposed to typing them. From there, think about the key points you want to have on the board and how you want them displayed. Use your creativity to have them aptly displayed, based on your likes.

Designate some time—say, five minutes each day—to gaze at this vision board, and soon enough, this will become second nature.

12. WRITING TO-DO LISTS

'Motivation gets you going, but discipline keeps you growing.'

—John C. Maxwell

One of the most important time management tools is a to-do list—that list you require to get things done. It is as simple as its underlying rationale. A to-do list puts all your tasks in one place, and from there, you can prioritize and tackle the important ones first. This concept may be simple, but it does have crucial advantages which can bring great changes in your life.

It's a Reminder

Our brains are not the best memory tools, and they only trust systems they believe work like to-do lists. Having a properly written list will help you remember when you need to do things, so that you do not miss anything. Having such lists makes you more relaxed and focused on things. You don't have to struggle to ensure you don't forget something important when you have a to-do list that remembers everything for you.

It Assists You in Setting Priorities and Completing Tasks Systematically

When you create a list, you naturally highlight important tasks or write them in order of priority. This helps you focus on those items that are most important as opposed to working on the less significant items when you get tempted to do that (because the latter are much easier to do). When you've got a list of stuff you need to do, you decide the kind of jobs you should do first, and things get completed according to their urgency and importance as you move down your list.

It Allows You to Coordinate the Same Tasks

A major problem we usually have is repeating things which waste a lot of time. For instance, if you have to feed your cat and leash your dog—both of which stay in the same area—a to-do list tells you to do these tasks together.

We know that so much time gets lost in stopping, starting and switching between different types or levels of activity. By doing some tasks together, you could save a lot of time. I mean, you buy all the things you require at the same time, reply to all the messages on multiple platforms or even complete all your errands in a single run. Doesn't that make you more efficient with your time?

You Get to Track Your Progress

With to-do lists, you are better able to follow up on things you have set out to do. Such lists let you mark off the activities you've completed, and, at the end of the day, looking at the list gives you a sense of satisfaction and accomplishment. A to-do list could also wake you up if you had gone to bed with something on it that was left unmarked!

Exercise

Take a few minutes each day before you go to bed and write down the five most important tasks that you have to complete the following day. These things should be ones that will give you the greatest satisfaction and are crucial to accomplishing your goals.

Note: Ensure that your to-do list is not too long, because if it is, it will serve to only overwhelm you rather than motivate you to get things done.

13. JOURNALING

'Journal writing gives us insights into who we are, who we were, and who we can become.'

—Sandra Marinella

Throughout history, successful people have kept journals. We have state leaders who have preserved them for posterity and other famous individuals who have done the same for their own purposes.

According to Oscar Wilde, a playwright of the nineteenth century, a journal is necessary: *'I never travel without my diary. One should always have a sensational piece to read on the train.'*

Writing itself accesses the left-brain region, which is rational and analytical. While the left-brain region is engaged, the right brain is free to build, feel and intuit. Writing generally removes the mental blocks and lets you use all your brain power to understand yourself better, as well as other people and the world around you. In summary, these are some of the benefits you get by journaling.

- *You Have Clarity of Thought and Feelings*
  Sometimes we get all jumbled up within us, not sure what we feel or want. When you take a couple of minutes to write down your emotions and thoughts, you get in touch with your inner self quickly. Everything inside becomes clear.
- *You Get to Know Yourself Better*
  When you make it a routine to write, you get to understand what makes you confident and happy. You also become clear about individuals and situations that are lethal to you; all this is critical information to improve your emotional well-being.
- *You Have Less Stress*
  A habit of writing about sadness, anger and other emotions that can cause pain assists you in decreasing the intensity of such feelings. You also get to feel calmer and develop a better ability to stay in the present.
- *You Are Able to Solve Problems More Effectively*
  We typically solve problems from an analytical (left-brained) perspective. Sometimes, though, the answer can only be found by involving the intuition and creativity of the right-brain area. Writing works to unlock these other important capabilities and gives you the chance to find unexpected solutions to what would otherwise seem to be unsolvable problems.

Exercise

Purchase a journal or a diary, and each day, take about twenty minutes to record your thoughts and feelings about your life. You can begin anywhere. Just remember that there are no rules here!

This book has been updated with ninety-nine questions and launched as a journal titled *Know Thyself*. You can purchase it on Amazon.

14. PRACTISING POSITIVE AFFIRMATIONS

'Certain people think they will feel good if certain things happen. The trick is: You have to feel good for no reason.'

—Richard Bandler

By definition, self-affirmations are statements that you would tell yourself with an aim to spark self-change. We use them to change our beliefs about ourselves and to make them more positive.

In general, self-affirmations work as a vital part of the psychological immune system. For instance, when your supervisor at work criticizes your job too harshly, you can give yourself positive reminders such as 'it's all fine, it's going to be okay', to assist you in handling the situation.

Even though we tend to use self-affirmations as a way to cope, they can also serve as our motivation.

Simply put, when we feel good about ourselves, we are more likely to take action, as compared to when we do not feel good about ourselves. Thus, by telling ourselves things like 'I love my job', we feel great about going to work. Conversely, when we feel bad about ourselves, we automatically become complacent, miserable and at a higher risk of developing health problems.

Benefits of Having Daily Affirmations

Businessman and author Robert Kiyosaki said: *'It's not what you say out of your mouth that determines your life, it's what you whisper to yourself that has the most power.'*

Affirmations are basically more than just self-help statements to make yourself feel better. They can have a great impact on the overall quality of your life. Regular affirmations let you become more in tune with your thoughts and how you think about yourself.

When you become conscious of your attitude towards the self, you can make an effort to eliminate negative thoughts. When you are better aware of yourself, you become more mindful of surrounding yourself with positive things.

Actually, the more you practise, the more you realize which aspects of your life are most important to you and other things that could be impeding your happiness. What's more, daily affirmations can put you in a steady, positive mood. As an optimistic person, you tend to be healthier, more productive and happier than if you view yourself cynically.

Last but not least, having daily affirmations will allow you to have a clearer perspective of the obstacles you are bound to face in life. In other words, if you practise daily affirmations, you are better able to avoid worrying about little things, because you already have a better grasp of what's important in your life. You are able to think about the bigger picture and don't easily get overwhelmed by trivial annoyances.

Exercise

Create your daily affirmations and write them down. Note that it's not enough to say positive things about yourself aloud. It is only when you write them down that you can increase their potency. These affirmations should generally have the following characteristics:

- They need to be stated positively and in the present. For instance, *'I am achieving this'* or *'I am beautiful'* or *'I am healthy'*.
- They have to be instantly gratifying to be effective.
- They have to be unconditional. Thus, 'I will achieve this if I get promoted' is not right because it suggests that a condition needs to be met first for you to benefit.

Some examples of good affirmations are as follows:

- I am strong
- I am enough
- I get better every day
- I am proud of myself
- I am in charge of my life

15. TAKING SHORT NAPS

'The nap is a sort of easy version of meditation.'

—Tom Hodgkinson

Recently, there has been a growing negative perception of napping, and it has slowly become deeply ingrained in American culture. When most people think of napping, their minds immediately shift to someone carelessly passed out on the floor after having eaten a giant sandwich. Naps are looked at as a practice for the unambitious and lazy, or for retirees who have a lot of time on their hands.

Today, many Americans do not like taking breaks. Most of them are even using their vacation time to accomplish more things. They go on to down endless cups of coffee, along with energy drinks and supplements, to become more efficient throughout the day.

Nonetheless, taking short naps during the day is a highly overlooked option that could alleviate daytime drowsiness. This practice enhances performance, improves alertness and has other benefits such as:

- *It Improves Memory and Learning Ability*
  Napping basically improves your working memory. This is the kind of memory that is typically engaged when you're working on intricate tasks, where you have to focus on one thing out of the many other things that you hold in your memory. Napping also boosts your retention of memory. When you sleep, your recent memories are taken to an area in the brain known as the neocortex, which cements and stores all long-term memories.

- *It Improves Mood*
  Serotonin, the neurotransmitter we've already invoked in the context of various habits, also plays a role here as a mood and sleep regulator. You know that it offers a feeling of contentment and well-being. When our bodies get stressed out, we have higher levels of serotonin being used rapidly and the production of more gets blocked. In consequence, we become depressed, anxious, overwhelmed, easily distracted and irritable. Napping sort of bathes your brain in this neurotransmitter, to reverse those effects and create a more positive mood.

- *It Increases Your Creativity and Alerts the Senses*
  Napping is able to boost your sensory perception as effectively as sleeping at night. This simply means that, as a result, the music you like begins to sound more melodious, the eggs taste better and the sunrise looks prettier.

- ***It Helps Improve Your Health***
  Sleep deprivation leads to an excess of the hormone
  known as cortisol in the body. Cortisol is known
  as the stress hormone and helps us fuel our flight-
  or-fight instinct in a crisis. However, when you
  have too much of this hormone in your system, you
  experience high glucose intolerance and increased
  abdominal fat, and a weakened immune and
  muscular system.

  Furthermore, it causes problems in learning
  and memory, and reduces the level of testosterone
  and growth hormones in the body. As you would
  expect, this brings about adverse effects which
  can lead to issues like heart disease and diabetes.
  Regular napping sorts this out for you without
  your noticing it.

Exercise

Make a point of having a short nap at least once every
day. Experts assert that the standard nap time should
be around thirty minutes and should be taken between
1 p.m. and 3 p.m. During this time, and especially
with a ninety-minute nap, you will have an optimal
balance of all the various stages of sleep. In this nap,
you'll have the ratio of the sleep stages reflecting that
of normal nocturnal sleep.

Definitely, though, you may not have up to an hour
and a half to spend on your nap during the day. You
might, therefore, want to tailor your nap according to
your particular needs on a given day.

16. CARRYING A WATER BOTTLE

How much water are you drinking per day? Do you achieve the recommended daily capacity, or are you like most Americans who are far from getting close to it?

In 2013, a study found that 78 per cent of people don't drink more than eight cups per day, with 7 per cent going a full day without drinking any water at all. This study was conducted by the National Cancer Institute's Food Attitudes and Behavior wing.

Your body is made up of about 60 per cent water, and thus, to ensure that there is no fluid imbalance, you should develop a habit of drinking water regularly. This will assist in transporting nutrients across the body, digesting food and regulating body temperature, just to mention a few benefits.

It is, however, difficult to remember to drink as much water as you require. That's why ensuring that you always have a water bottle with you helps.

Following are some of the benefits of carrying a water bottle at all times or drinking water regularly.

- *It Helps You Lose Weight*
  Drinking a lot of water tends to delay hunger pangs, reduces the cravings that occur randomly and improves the body's metabolism. There are studies that have also proven that people who increase their intake of water during their weight-loss dieting plan lose more weight than people who do not drink as much water.

  If you think about it, when you are on the go and feel thirsty, you will always have something on hand right away. Thus, you won't be tempted to indulge in a soda from the closest outlet. If you are having serious sugar cravings, you can add fruit to your water for a healthy drink that quenches your thirst as well.

- *It Reduces Chances of Stroke and Risk of Heart Attack*
  Getting enough hydration prevents blood clots that can easily jeopardize the supply of oxygen in your body. It also ensures that the excess salt is excreted from the body and blood pressure is normalized, thus reducing the risk of the above-mentioned conditions.

- *It Improves Skin Health*
  Your skin is the largest organ you have. Drinking water regularly improves your skin's texture and elasticity. By keeping yourself hydrated, you help the skin sweat properly to regulate body temperature.

- *It Strengthens Your Joints*
  Water ensures that the cartilage around the joints is kept soft and hydrated. When the cartilage is hydrated, your joints are able to move with ease. Water, in this case, helps in lubricating the body's joints.
- *It Prevents Headaches and Helps You Stay Alert*
  Besides causing muscle fatigue, lack of water leads to headaches and reduces the capacity of the brain to retain short-term memory.

'Being continually dehydrated reduces your body's blood capacity, forcing your heart to pump more to be able to deliver the cells containing oxygen to your body muscles. When you are just becoming seriously dehydrated, you may become irritable, dizzy and have headaches. As you become more dehydrated, you become exhausted and clumsy, your eyesight fades and as you become severely dehydrated, you may feel nauseous and start vomiting. Without water, you could easily enter a coma and die.'

—Anonymous

Drinking water frequently averts all this, and helps you remain alert and focused.

Drinking water regularly and generally ensuring that your body is properly hydrated can help in ensuring optimal mental functioning and growth of cognitive abilities. It can also help you to keep your energy levels up during the day.

Exercise

Have your own water bottle and take it everywhere you go.

Also, instead of purchasing a plastic bottle every other day, you could consider getting a shatterproof glass bottle to help you stay committed and environment-friendly. Also, disposable plastic bottles usually have chemicals, such as BPA, that can easily get into your water. Glass does not have any chemicals and is reusable.

17. WALK MORE OFTEN AND GET A FITNESS BAND

Walking is a simple activity that you have been undertaking since you were very young. It is the 'closest thing there is to a wonder drug', according to Dr Thomas Frieden, former director of the Center for Disease Control and Prevention.

But definitely, you already know that any form of physical activity which includes walking is a plus to your overall health. But walking as an activity is in particular associated with myriads of benefits, some of which are listed below.

Better Mood

According to research, regular walking slowly modifies your entire nervous system so intensely that you get to experience a reduction in feelings of hostility and anger. This gets better when you are doing social walks, with friends, neighbours or acquaintances.

That sort of interaction makes you feel connected, and, as a result, your mood really improves.

Making a habit of walking outdoors regularly exposes you to natural sunlight, which can assist you in staving off what is known as the seasonal affective disorder or SAD, thus making the activity a great potential antidote for the cold, dark winter blues.

Boosts Your Memory

While exercise is good for the brain, walking, in particular, is great when it comes to boosting your memory. A study published in the *Proceedings of the National Academy of Sciences* in 2011 proved that walking even for forty minutes can increase the volume of the brain region associated with memory, known as the hippocampus, by 2 per cent, which is quite significant.

In 2014, another study was presented at the American Association for the Advancement of Science's annual meeting, which showed that taking regular brisk walks can slow down a shrinking brain and the waning of mental skills usually brought about by old age. This particular study was conducted with both women and men between the ages of sixty and eighty, and its conclusion was that by taking a short walk three times a week, you can increase the size of that brain area associated with memory and planning.

Boosts Your Immunity

Going by the many studies being conducted today, we have seen that moderately paced walks, taking about thirty minutes each day, can increase the number of immune system cells in the body. The overall effect of this is that the body's ability to fight diseases is remarkably enhanced, thus keeping you healthier.

Great for Old Age

Walking from an early age has also been proven to be one of the best things you can do for yourself, as it enables you to stay independent and mobile when you are old. Many studies state that adults who exercise regularly are significantly less likely to become disabled or suffer any episode of physical disability.

Exercise

First, make sure you walk at least thirty minutes every day, preferably in the morning.

Second, you will need to get yourself a fitness tracker to monitor your health and activity (without making any effort), and to know how you are doing. A fitness tracker or band is simply a kind of 'electronic finger on your pulse' that measures all the important factors, including your step count, with unmatched accuracy.

18. HAVING A DAILY QUESTIONNAIRE

Benjamin Franklin started and ended each of his days with a question. In the morning, he would ask himself, 'What good will I do today?' And in the evening, he would ask himself, 'What good have I done today?'

As a matter of fact, most great thinkers we know embraced the idea of ceaselessly questioning things, and themselves. As Albert Einstein would say, *'Learn from yesterday, live for today, hope for tomorrow. The important thing is not to stop questioning.'*

Definitely, thinking of practising self-reflection is much easier than actually doing it, since we are often inclined to avoid asking ourselves the hard and difficult questions.

John Dewey, a philosopher and psychologist, asserted in his book *How We Think* (1910) that self-reflection involves overcoming our tendency to just look and accept things as they are, as well as the willingness to tolerate mental unrest.

When we endure this discomfort, it results in an increase in confidence, which is important in performing better in work and day-to-day life.

Daily questionnaires, or getting into the habit of asking yourself questions every day, helps you to know whether you are living up to your fullest potential. Take a look at the following questionnaires, which can be used during the morning and before going to bed.

Morning Questionnaire

1. How am I going to make the most of my day?
2. What is the agenda for the day?
3. Did I meditate and exercise?
4. What are the top three priorities of the day?
5. How will I celebrate once they are accomplished?

Night Questionnaire

1. Did I have fun today?
2. How effective was I today?
3. What did I learn today?
4. How can I be more effective tomorrow?

Exercise

Write down your own set of questions and keep the note with you or stick it near your bed. Ask yourself these questions every day to track your progress.

19. SAYING THANK YOU

'If the only prayer you said was thank you, that would be enough.'

—Meister Eckhart

Whether it's an act of appreciating a worker's completion of a task, a customer's decision to purchase your product or continue using your services, or a child's effort in completing a chore, the simple act of saying 'thank you' shows appreciation and a recognition of what someone has done. It is more than good manners, and it's incredibly important.

We are taught to say 'thank you' for gifts, for special favours, for any assistance we receive in times of need. But it's not just in relation to the big things that it matters to say thank you. We also say thank you when we receive change at a store, when a person holds open a door for us, or when someone passes the salt to you at lunch. This phrase is thus quite ubiquitous, and it's ever welcome. You know that it can mean so much to people. But do you say thank you enough?

How Much Do You Say It?

Do you only say thank you to the people you love, or to those you are looking to impress or deem important? Can you remember any one time you received exceptional service at a store or restaurant, or any other place like that, and you felt bad because you didn't remember to say thank you? Or perhaps you did not take a moment to say thank you properly to someone? How often have you felt cross or resentful when another person went without saying thank you to you? 'She should have at least thanked me!' you might have thought. Or, 'How impolite! He couldn't even bother to say thank you!'

I'm sure you've heard many social commentators bemoaning how people who don't say 'thank you' are rude. Lynne Truss, in her book *Talk to the Hand: The Utter Bloody Rudeness of the World Today*, refers to the modest 'thank you' as one of the best weapons we have to stem the problem of rudeness.

What It Means

The message is very clear. When you neglect or forget to say 'thank you', you are perceived as being rude; not only does it annoy and upset people around you, it makes you look bad. You might be very busy or important, but it is always good to thank people regardless of the magnitude of what they have done for you.

When you wonder why saying 'thank you' is important, ask yourself why you feel so hurt or even let down when someone is not appreciative of you. Saying 'thank you' is not merely an empty ritual or a meaningless reflex.

As a matter of fact, it has something that is truly magical about it. These are just words, like 'sorry', but these words tend to act as a shorthand for a lot more. 'Thank you' conveys gratitude and shows your appreciation. Beyond that, it is a sign of respect for the person who helped you or gave you something. It is a way of showing that you are not taking them for granted and an acknowledgement that they truly matter. That's pretty much the reason why saying 'thank you' matters so much.

What Are Some of the Rewards of Saying 'Thank You'?

You know that saying 'thank you' truly matters to the people you say it to, but it can have some awesome rewards for you, too. You can surely get a long way without saying it, but with it you can get a lot further.

For starters, as a person who makes a habit of saying 'thank you', you get better service. What's more, you'll often find that people are willing and ready to go the extra mile on your behalf. Definitely, you know that showing gratitude in this way to friends, colleagues or family will end in positive payback in all sorts of ways—from increased business success to a happier home life. Actually, many business gurus will tell you that the secret of their success is always taking the time to say 'thank you'. It may not come as so much of a surprise to you when I tell you that studies are repeatedly affirming that thanks and appreciation are, in most cases, a bigger motivator in America than a pay rise!

Exercise

Learn to say 'thank you' in as many instances as you can. But wait . . . Do you even know how to *properly* say 'thank you'? I mean, it is surprising how many people get it wrong nowadays, if not failing entirely at it! I will give you the four simple but important steps of saying these magic words in person, effectively and successfully.

- Make sure you appear sincere by making eye contact
- Smile
- In a friendly voice, try saying the words clearly, don't mutter
- Tell the person what you are thanking them for (be specific)

  Let's look at some examples:

- I thank you for helping me with this
- I thank you for the great piece of advice
- I thank you for letting me stay the night

If you are thanking a person whose name you know for sure, you can address them by name to make it sound better: 'Jane, thank you for the delicious dinner.'

Secondly, if you know the person rather too well, and if it is appropriate, you can include a light touch on their arm, a hug or even a kiss.

20. STANDING AND WORKING

Sitting has been linked to problems usually associated with sedentary lifestyles, such as poor metabolic health, increased risk of heart disease as well as cognitive and memory loss. This is why you'll often hear sitting being dubbed 'the new smoking'.

Sometime back, a small study was published in a journal known as *PLOS ONE*. It suggested that sitting down for too long may contribute to cognitive problems and memory loss. This study looked at thirty-five working adults who were between the ages of forty-five and seventy-five. Their brain scans were taken to measure the thickness of the medial temporal lobe (MTL) of each person. The MTL is the part of the brain that is particularly important in memory.

In this study, each person was asked about how much time they spent deskbound and moving around per day. According to the research, though, it wasn't possible to identify a clear cause–effect relationship, but the researchers did find that increased sedentary time was linked with the decreasing thickness of the MTL, something which suggests that sitting for long periods could put you in danger of developing cognitive disorders.

There was another study that involved ten office workers. They stood for 180 minutes after lunch, throughout the span of the study, and the results were amazing: their blood sugar spike reduced by 43 per cent.

When it comes to well-being, standing desks have been seen to have a positive effect overall. In a separate study, spanning seven weeks, participants who used standing desks reported that they felt less fatigued and stressed out as compared to those who had remained seated during the entire workday.

Lastly, standing while working improves energy and mood. A study shows how these factors, linked to the use of a standing desk, help in boosting productivity.

However, when you consider studies like the one that was published in the journal *Ergonomics*, which states that it may not be healthy to spend long hours standing on your feet, deciding whether to work standing or sitting may become a little bit complicated.

This study found that standing for too long during the workday could lead to physical discomfort all over the body and make it more difficult to stay focused and energized. Thus, you may need to make a decision based on what suits you as an individual, as there is no one-size-fits-all solution. This means you must consider factors such as pregnancy, orthopaedic issues, physical fitness and body weight, which could make you more or less suited to standing at work.

All in all, there is scientific evidence that supports the notion that we should aim to minimize the time we spend sitting as much as possible, which, according to me, is rather obvious.

Experts say that eating well and being active (which means less time spent sitting down) is important for the brain and body, and switching to a standing desk may help (especially when you have supportive shoes and have a soft mat to stand on, to reduce the strain on the joints and the back).

Exercise

First, you can improvise. Simply keep a box underneath your computer. If, however, you want to spend money on this, you can purchase standing desks which are out there in the market. Specific office furniture outlets offer really good sit–stand desks you could benefit from. Just remember that when you get one, you should begin by splitting your time equally between standing and sitting.

21. TALKING TO YOURSELF

'Be mindful of your self talk. It's a conversation with the universe.'

—David James Lees

I have a friend who says that if he didn't talk to himself, no one would listen to him. This sentiment could easily pass as cynical (comically), but there is a bit of truth to it.

When you talk through your thoughts, it can be really beneficial to your cognitive functioning and memory, and for your physical and mental health, just to mention a few benefits. You may definitely catch a few odd glares from people if they caught you talking to yourself, say, in public, but you should take lots of comfort in the fact that doing so is keeping you properly prepared for the stressful days you have to endure sometimes.

A study published in *Procedia* looked at the effects of the two common types of self-talk, which include instructional and motivational self-talk, on people playing basketball. It was discovered that players did pass the ball faster when they audibly motivated themselves through the task.

In another study, researchers claimed that even the way you refer to yourself when you are talking to yourself can make a difference. These researchers were studying the impact of internal self-talk—that is, talking to yourself in your mind—to find out how it affects feelings and attitudes. They saw that when their participants talked in the second or third person about themselves—for instance, 'John can do this' or 'You can do this'—they felt less anxious while doing it and got better ratings on their performance by their peers. This, according to the researchers, was a result of self-distancing—that is, focusing on yourself from the distanced perspective of another person, although this person is you.

Let me give you a simple example of why psychological distance helps. Recall a certain point in time when you were with a loved one or a friend thinking about a problem. As an outsider, it is quite simple for you to offer good advice to them for that particular problem. The main reason you are able to advise other people on a problem is that you are not sucked into those issues, and you are distanced from their experience—which pretty much makes you think more clearly.

Therefore, when you get frazzled and need a motivational pep talk, you could consider giving it either in the third or second person, which can help you look at the situation from an objective, logical perspective, instead of an emotional, subjective one.

Other Benefits

Apart from motivational self-talk, talking to yourself loudly in an instructional manner can really speed up your cognitive ability in terms of task performance and problem-solving. So, for instance, when you are searching for an item you cannot find in your library, you might do yourself some good by talking to yourself out loud. This is due to what is known as feedback hypothesis.

Researchers working on feedback hypothesis conducted a series of experiments in which they asked the participants to search for different objects in various situations. The subjects, in one experiment, were requested to look for a picture of a given item, such as a mango or banana, among twenty images of random items.

In this group there were participants who would say the object's name out loud to themselves. The participants who said the word 'banana' before they searched for a picture of the object found the picture quicker and more accurately. The study found that saying the word aloud made the participants more cognizant of its physical traits, which then made the banana photo stand out for them among photos of other objects.

This suggests that talking to yourself about what you are doing can make you stay focused. Researchers have concluded that motivational and positive self-talk works best on the tasks that are based on strength, speed and power, and instructional self-talk works best with tasks that involve strategy, focus and technique.

You can use self-talk on problems where you are trying to stay on task and there are likely distractions. When it comes to tasks that entail a multistep sequence, you can talk to yourself out loud to keep distractions out and remind yourself exactly where you are.

Exercise

Simply set some quality time for yourself to have a conversation with yourself, preferably every day.

22. HAVING ANCHOR WORDS

An anchor is simply a trigger that helps us retrieve a desired emotional state. It can take any form. For instance, a piece of music or a statement that stimulates or sort of brings out a particular emotion or feeling that is associated with something specific that you were doing (you could have been with someone you love, listening to a certain song); or something that generally motivates you to do something else (which you otherwise wouldn't have done without this motivation).

Anchoring is so powerful because you can remember any emotional state you want with it. You can also create an anchor for motivation. We need to motivate ourselves to stay on track. People unconsciously use certain words which help them to stay alert or stay on track. You can use words such as: 'You can, Daniel'; 'Come on, Daniel'; 'You are the best'; 'If not you, then who else?'

So how can you create anchor words? Let us find out.

Steps for Creating an Anchor

Before you think of any anchor words, you need to consider the three core things you need to create an anchor. These include the following.

Uniqueness

An anchor trigger needs to be unique. The main reason for this is that you wouldn't want the anchor to be weak. Simple!

Repetition

At first, when you create the trigger, you sort of need to stack the anchor, which means that the more times you set the trigger during the peak of your emotional state, the more the trigger becomes associated with the emotion, and the more it becomes effective for you.

Intensity

When you are creating your anchor, you need to do so at the top of your emotional intensity. Therefore, if the emotion you want to experience is absolute, as well as motivation and total empowerment, just get yourself to that state by recalling a time when you were in that particular state, or picture what it would be like to be in that state. For this kind of emotion and to increase the intensity, it would be a great idea to get your entire body involved.

Exercise

Create phrases which inspire you the most (using the steps above) or get you moving, and practise saying them to yourself when you feel down.

23. APPRECIATING OTHERS

From the time we were young, we have always been taught to use such words as 'thank you' and 'please'. We've been taught to appreciate what we have because it was much more than what others would ever have, and it was necessary to let the people who were helping us know how much what they were doing (even if not directly for us) meant to us. We've been taught to never open a present and appear unhappy or unappreciative. It is important to show appreciation to people who are always there, directly or indirectly, to help you, and others as well.

The amount of assistance people offer to you, which goes unnoticed, is simply incredible. Can you count the number of times a particular person has assisted you and you have not exactly given them the appreciation they probably deserve for the task they did? When you show appreciation for others, it makes it simpler for them to appreciate you in return. One of the main reasons people fail to show appreciation for others, for instance, is because they don't feel appreciated themselves.

You should know that being appreciated is good for others the same way it is for you. It helps you find yourself and your values.

Let's look at some reasons you should be showing appreciation to people around you.

Enables You to Build Self-Esteem

Do you remember the way it felt to get an ovation? Perhaps during your graduation or when you got an award, like the one for the spelling bee? You remember how good it felt, don't you? It made you feel like everything you worked for was worth it, and you got some sort of assurance that you did a really good job and that all the work you'd put in had paid off.

Well, it is a simple gesture, people just clapping their hands together; yet, the fulfilment it brings is simply unfathomable! When you develop the habit of expressing appreciation towards the people around you, and the people you meet when they do something or accomplish something, you make them more confident and willing to make the effort once more and do the same thing again, perhaps even at a larger scale.

People Become Motivated to Do Better

We have four key reasons why people nowadays quit their jobs. These include lack of empowerment, bad boss, office politics and, of course, lack of recognition or appreciation.

Unfortunately, nearly all companies suffer from these ills, and if you are unlucky enough, you'll get all four. We have numerous ways to motivate people at work. Most people I know regard appreciation from others as one of the factors they consider to stay on in some place and improve on what they had done.

Particularly if you are a leader, you need to make it a habit of showing appreciation towards your staff each time you get the chance. Even a simple 'well done' or 'good job' goes a long way, regardless of whether it is written or spoken.

People really need to know that their efforts are getting appreciated and that they are making significant contributions towards your goals. Being an employee, I find recognition necessary for me, and one of the things that I look for in a boss or a company is the ability to recognize other people's work. My desire is to work for a company that does not just care for profits. I never want to work for a person who is talking to his/her staff only to point out their mistakes.

It Shows How Much You Care

You should also make a point of giving credit where it is due. If you are a leader, you should make an effort to do so even more resoundingly. You'd be surprised how much people still talk about having the kind of boss who only engages with you when you slip up to rub it in your face; you know, the classic *fault-finder*. If you are a leader, whether in a company, a social group, in your family or wherever else, you need to consider that the people you are dealing with are not objects; they have feelings that need to be taken care of, and they are not your slaves.

It is for this reason that I appreciate the value of regular coaching in an organization where you talk to your staff directly, not just about work but also about their personal lives. This makes a leader more human in their eyes.

Exercise

Simply start appreciating the people around you more for the things they do, no matter how simple. It doesn't matter whether it's your friend, family, acquaintance or even your enemy. If you can't do it to make them happy, at least do it to make yourself happy.

24. LEARN TO CONTRIBUTE

While this is not something that we talk about often, and too many of us are engrossed in the so-called 'struggle' of our daily lives (rather too much to even think of contributing to individuals or communities around us), we still sincerely know, somewhere at the back of our minds, that there are too many people in society who are having a hard time.

Any contribution resonates with feelings of humanity, compassion and a sense of appreciation (especially if it's about giving back), and when we give to people, these feelings are awakened.

The kind of contribution I am talking about here, that you can offer to people or groups around you, is time, knowledge or financial contribution. This, you may note, should not be based on what you have in abundance, but merely on what you can afford to give, such as reading/writing material to schools, regular talks to social groups or facilitating such talks (by getting experts to do them or paying for the material), or something related to these.

In this world, there is simply nothing better to regain your focus than starting to understand how much you have to be grateful for. This comes from giving to people who are less fortunate than yourself.

Here are some of the reasons why you should consider contributing.

You Get Personal Satisfaction

Volunteering or giving back can be very rewarding. In some cases, you'll find yourself getting involved in projects that under normal circumstances you would not have got the chance to do.

When you make your contribution—say, a financial contribution—and the project is completed, you get a great feeling of satisfaction, from having contributed to, or just having helped produce something, that many people would benefit from.

Knowing that you helped many people come to an event where they learn about the latest techniques to help improve their lives will help you sleep better. In a small way, you pushed the community forward!

Alleviates Poverty and Suffering

On a very practical level, in finding ways to give back to society you are helping provide some sort of instant relief from poverty and suffering. Even while you might notice that a long-term, sustainable solution to such problems is required, people will still need food, clothes and access to basic sanitation immediately, which you can offer. You can actually do this in many ways, which include donating to a cause, teaching in seminars on ways of helping the underprivileged manage their situation or purchasing what they need to get by for a given period of time.

Builds Confidence

We all have areas in which we are not exactly brimming with confidence. When you start helping other people through contributions, you feel good about yourself, and it boosts your confidence. You are also able to work with different people, which also helps you grow in this regard.

You Grow and Challenge Yourself

When you work with a group of different people, whom you normally wouldn't choose to work with, it can come as a challenge to you. Deciding to start the life of interacting with the less fortunate can be difficult, even frustrating at times. When you really think about it, though, it is equally fantastic, because it gives you a chance to learn and grow as a person, and not just be there as a mindless, sheltered zombie who's probably churning out the usual nine-to-five work, with nothing else going on in his/her life. Anything that challenges you should be taken positively and boldly.

Exercise

Do your homework. First, determine what kind of knowledge you can give and in what form, or the amount of money you can regularly donate to make someone's life more bearable somewhere. Second, find groups or people around you that openly need such assistance and start helping.

25. MINI-BREAKS

Well, just about every one of us knows that we need to take regular breaks, but we always tell ourselves that there's a better way of doing things, or we are so busy we don't even think there is time to take a break. We thus keep going, as always.

Most working people see things this way until they discover the power of taking breaks. That is when they become more focused, happier and more productive. And you, too, can experience the same if you have this problem. There are real benefits of taking breaks that are supported by science. Let's take a look.

You Get Less Bored and Become More Focused

Picture this: you get in the groove of a project or task, and the ideas begin flowing; you feel great. But it only goes on for so long. You stretch yourself a little beyond your productivity zone and you start feeling zoned out, unfocused and even irritable. What is happening?

Apparently, the human brain is not built for the drawn-out focus we ask of it nowadays. The brain is vigilant at all times because it evolved to detect many different changes to make sure we survive. Therefore, focusing too much on one thing for too long is not something you are ever going to be great at. But the good news is that the fix for this problem is simple: all you need is a slight interruption (or a break) to get yourself back on track.

When you deactivate and reactivate your goals, you are able to remain focused. Practically speaking, research suggests that when you undertake long tasks, like studying before a big exam, you should have brief breaks. Short mental breaks actually assist you in staying focused on your task.

You Are Better Able to Re-evaluate Your Goals

According to *Harvard Business Review*, taking breaks will allow you to take a step back and ensure that you accomplish the right things, in the right manner. When you work continuously on a task, it is easy to lose focus and lose yourself in the weeds. Conversely, when you follow a brief intermission, you have to pick up where you left off, which in itself helps you take a while to just think globally about what you are really trying to achieve. This is a practice that pushes you to remain mindful of your objectives.

You Retain Information

Studies have proven that when our minds wander (while on a break), activity in most brain regions increases.

Studies have also shown that the mind tends to solve its stickiest problems in this state (daydreaming), and that you have breakthroughs, which seem to come out of nowhere, through this kind of *diffuse-mode* thinking.

The reason is that the relaxation that is normally associated with daydream mode lets the brain hook up and take back important insights. On the other hand, when you are focusing, you tend to block your access to this diffuse mode of thinking, which, according to scientists, is important in solving difficult and new problems.

Exercise

Take short breaks in any kind of work you do, particularly if it involves a lot of mental strain.

CONCLUSION

We have come to the end of the book. Thank you for reading, and congratulations on reading until the end.

Twenty-five habits may seem like *a lot* when you are just getting started with them. However, with time, dedication and commitment, they will become part of you, and you won't even notice you have absorbed them!

If you found the book valuable, can you recommend it to others? One way to do that is to post a review on Amazon.

Thank you and good luck!